HUMA

Its Culture and Moral Confusions

Howard Taylor

Sponsored by
The Scottish Order of Christian Unity

the *WayMark* series

Series Editor: David C Searle

Published by
Rutherford House

British Library Cataloguing in Publication Data

A catalogue record for this book is available from
The British Library

ISBN 1-904429-00-9

Typeset by David Searle, Edinburgh
and Printed by
T.J. International Ltd., Padstow, Cornwall

CONTENTS

FOREWORD

by

Lord Mackay of Clashfern, KT, PC, FRSE

After the Second World War and the disclosures of how Nazi Germany had treated its own citizens, particularly the Jews, the European nations and indeed the whole international community were so shocked that consideration was given to mechanisms that would prevent such occurrences in the future. Out of this consideration came the treaties that defined human rights to which individuals were entitled and which the states of which they were citizens were bound to protect.

These were constructed as treaties between states but soon it was realized that individuals should be afforded the right to claim against their own state if that state infringed those rights.

Although the obligations contained in these treaties were obligations on the states it was obvious that they carried implications as to the way in which citizens within the states should treat one another.

Having been contained in treaties these obligations also came to be enshrined in domestic law, sometimes as part of a written constitution, and sometimes as part of domestic legislation.

As a party to the European Convention on Human Rights and Fundamental Freedoms with its enforcing authorities in Strasbourg, the United Kingdom for many years acknowledged the rights of citizens complaining of human rights breaches to bring individual petitions. Following on from this, in 1998 the Human Rights Act was passed making these rights enforceable in the courts of this country.

The way in which these rights were expressed was a matter of negotiation between the parties to the treaties describing them. *But do they have any higher authority? How do these descriptions fit into the morality of human beings?* Do they have religious significance? For those of us who believe in God do they have divine authority?

In the account in the biblical book of Exodus of the giving of the Law to Israel, we have an account of the obligations of human beings to one another in the fifth to the tenth commandments. These are very simple direct statements, summarized by the Lord Jesus, in the second commandment 'Thou shalt love thy neighbour as thyself.'

The relationship between divine authority and the appropriate statement of relationships between human beings and between individuals and the state is the subject Howard Taylor addresses in this book. It is a fascinating and important subject, for the authority under which one human being acts towards another must be a vital ingredient in establishing the lawfulness of these acts. But even more, if the relationship between human beings should be based on love and respect for one another, as Jesus teaches, a motivation is provided for observing human rights which is much more powerful than observance of laws or obligations presented by merely human authority.

ACKNOWLEDGEMENTS

I am very grateful to Lord MacKay (formerly Lord Chancellor) for honouring this little book with a Foreword. I also acknowledge the help of Dr Henry Haslam in his helpfully critical comments about the preface; the encouragement of Dr Thomas Torrance and the careful editing of Revs David Torrance, David Searle and Mrs Alison Carter. However I take full responsibility for any imperfections in the actual text.

I am also immensely grateful to the *Scottish Order of Christian Unity* for sponsoring this book and for contributing towards its production by Rutherford House.

Howard Taylor
Edinburgh
May 2004

PREFACE

> A liberty or a civil right which does not explicitly or implicitly recognize responsibility to a morality which transcends the right is a mere arrogant assumption, based on selfishness and nothing else.[1]

The modern Human Rights movement gained world-wide momentum after the appalling atrocities of the Nazi era, especially the Nazi treatment of the Jewish people. No doubt those who drafted the United Nations Declaration of Human Rights were aroused by their belief that good and evil really exist and that humanity needs to be protected from evil. This protection is needed not only with reference to unrepresentative dictators but also with reference to majorities who cannot always be trusted not to persecute minorities in their midst. Even if the minority is just one human being, his/her life must be respected.

This leads inevitably to the problem of how to balance the general good with the individual good of a particular person. Older utilitarian theories of ethics (the 'good' is that which provides the greatest happiness of the greatest number) put the general good before the 'rights' of the individual. We return to this difficulty later. Putting the difficulty aside for the time being, we can be sure that many of those

---

[1] Lord Hailsham, Lord Chancellor and head of the British legal system from 1970-74 and 1979-87.

drafting the UN Human Rights Charter, consciously or unconsciously, would have been motivated by the Bible's teaching that human life is of great value to God, not just because of his creation but also because of his saving love shown in the sufferings and resurrection of Christ for us—a saving love to which the whole Bible story bears witness. Assuming this to be so, the impetus behind the formulation of the UN declaration could not, then, have been selfishness or a desire to dominate others. Almost certainly, they themselves were men and women who were comfortably well off, enjoying the 'rights' that they sought for all other people.

The purpose of this booklet is not to examine the 'rights' legislation in detail but to appraise the meaning of—and perils behind—the concept as it has developed in our contemporary culture.

The danger we face today is that this concept of 'human rights' is being cut off from a higher, transcendent Real Goodness so that it takes on a life of its own, becoming its own 'god'—there being nothing else by which to assess it. Being broken away from God, the concept of human rights may actually bring great harm to humanity, enabling the powerful to impose their desires on the weak through their domination of politics and especially the media. Both the multi-faith philosophy of the current age, together with the practical privatization of religion (religion is only for those who like that sort of thing) means that there can be no publicly agreed purpose for human life and therefore no public agreement about the value of human life. Medical ethics, especially that dealing with genetics, is just one example of how, without an anchor, ethics becomes an ever-shifting sand.

Assessing good and evil

Yet instinctively governments and people recognize that there has to be some overarching means of judging good and evil. For many it will be the big idea of human rights. However, in some contexts there may be other big ideas.

For example, in the lead-up to the 2003 Iraq War there was enormous controversy in the Western world as to the rightness or wrongness of the proposed invasion. What was intriguing was the widespread belief expressed in opinion polls and by certain prominent politicians that if the United Nations Security Council would give its approval, then the invasion would be right, and if not it would be wrong. The United Nations became for many the sole means of justifying or condemning the war. This was so, even though it was well known that the members of the Security Council included tyrannical dictatorships and that the means of persuading individual security council members to vote one way or the other included bribery and threats—from the big hitters on both sides of the argument.

There are three ways in which the concept of human rights is in danger of either becoming its own 'god' or of dehumanizing ethical discussion.

First, human rights legislation is becoming the sole means of judging the rightness or wrongness of the legislation of national governments.

This has been a gradual process and is certainly not all bad. There are two courts that are relevant here.

First, in the mid 20th century the European Court of Human Rights based in Strasbourg was set up and given the power to determine whether or not acts of any parliament contravene the European Convention on Human Rights which was formulated soon after the Second World War. This Court has the power to declare that acts of parliament or government contravene the Convention. Although the British Government can ignore its findings, in individual cases, the Court can still award damages against the government.

Second there is the European Court of Justice based in Luxembourg. This is a court of the European Union (EU). The EU decided to incorporate the Convention on Human Rights into its constitution and this is the Court that can rule whether acts of various parliaments contravene this Convention. While Britain is a member of the EU, this Court's decisions take precedence over British Acts of Parliament.

In 1998 the British Parliament passed the Human Rights Act which enabled British courts to decide whether or not British laws contravene the European Convention on Human Rights. British Courts cannot annul Acts of Parliament but if they do declare an Act of Parliament in contravention of the Convention then Parliament has to meet to decide what to do.

Now we ponder this question. What are we doing when in ordinary discussion we say that such and such a law is just or unjust? We are implicitly appealing to a higher sense of justice by which we judge the rightness or wrongness of legislation. This higher Goodness is not a list of rules, rights or responsibilities. It is not measurable. Nevertheless we believe it is something real and hence we can have a rational debate about the morality of the government policies which we are discussing. The danger is that with the demise of a definite belief in such a transcendent Goodness, human constructs such as 'human rights' legislation take the place of God as the source of our knowledge of right and wrong. *But in a world of competing rights who is to decide which rights are more right?* Obviously the strong, those with influence, the media, the politicians and the judges will make the decision.

Second, there is a growing human rights culture where each is encouraged to claim his/her rights.
This tendency inevitably leads to the atomization of society into a world of competing rights. For most

people in Britain it has not gone that far. However the trends are real and growing.

At this point I can do no better than refer to parts of the Preface to Mary Ann Glendon's highly acclaimed book, *Rights Talk*.[2] In it she is explicitly criticizing the American 'rights talk'. However I believe that much of what she says is becoming relevant to this side of the Atlantic. She complains about its 'legalistic character, its exaggerated absoluteness, its hyper-individualism, its insular-ity, and its silence with respect to personal, civic and collective responsibilities'. Further on in the Preface she says:

> A tendency to frame nearly every social controversy in terms of a clash of rights (a woman's right to her own body vs. a fetus's right to life) impedes compromise, mutual understanding, and the discovery of common ground.

> Converging with the language of psychotherapy, rights talk encourages our all-too-human tendency to place the self at the center of our moral universe.

In her first chapter she goes on to warn that

> the language of rights is the language of no compromise. The winner takes all and the loser has to get out of town. The conversation is over.[3]

---

[2] The Free Press.
[3] *Rights Talk*, p.9.

Human rationality stifled

Third, the great number of regulations based on the concept of human rights tends to stifle human rationality.

Committees in public life, especially those that are expected to have an ethical dimension, should have reasoned discussions about what should be encouraged because it is right and what should be avoided because it is wrong. However, more and more such committees are dominated by the question, What is the legislation forcing us to do? More and more institutions are aware that they need to 'watch their back' because there will always be some who are looking for an excuse to sue.

Although lists of human rights in the European Union and United Nations may not be hugely long, how to interpret those rights into the enormous variety of circumstances in which humans find themselves, inevitably leads to the multiplication of a never-ending stream of regulations. Thus committees, which should be engaged in rational discussion about how 'right' and 'wrong' should affect decisions, are forced instead to seek expertise in a mass of regulations. However, as we shall see, Real Goodness is necessarily transcendent and personal and therefore not measurable or exactly definable. It is precisely this that makes human reason and discussion necessary.

Writing about the nature of goodness, justice and morality, Lord Hailsham says:

The fact that these things are not measurable, calculable, or verifiable explains much, perhaps all, of the argument. But the fact that they remain objective realities proves that the argument is not about nothing. A law which does not appeal to the *rational* in man is no better than a stick or a carrot applied to a donkey, by whomsoever or whatsoever it is passed.[4] (Emphasis added.)

My contention

This book argues that

- a Real Goodness exists quite independent of our human opinions, preferences and formulations and thus we must assume there is also a Real Morality
- nevertheless this Real Morality does impinge upon our human lives and this is the explanation of what we commonly call our 'conscience'
- the only explanation for this can be a transcendent reality, which is good and the ultimate source of all goodness; whether people recognize it or not, this is the ultimate origin of the human conviction that right and wrong really exist
- our relationship with that transcendent reality is all-important
- it is not unreasonable to believe that this transcendent reality is the God of the Bible
- Real Goodness cannot be described in mere legal terms but needs a deeply personal revelation

---

[4] This is taken from a fuller quotation from *The Door Wherein I Went*, p.64, given later in the text on p. 52.

- although humanity in general is aware of this goodness, it is not unreasonable to believe that it is fully revealed in the life, death and resurrection of Jesus Christ who personally embodies the self-giving love of God and provides the guarantee that evil and suffering are temporary whilst faith, hope and love abide forever

- the laws and commandments of God are still needed because, in our imperfect world, an as yet imperfect fellowship with, and therefore knowledge of Christ, limits our knowledge and wisdom

- attempts to replace the God of the Bible with 'human rights' are doomed to failure because:

  - this concept contains its own inner contradictions and leads to moral confusion

  - in the long term, such inner contradictions will be used as an excuse for the exploitation of the weak by the strong and those without influence by the influential

  - these exploitations are the very reverse of the original intentions of this concept

- the doctrine of 'natural rights', derived from the belief in a good God and a good Creation, is insufficient of itself to provide a moral framework for our relationships

- the gospel of the redeeming love of God is also needed

CHAPTER 1

INTRODUCTION

Responsibility and accountability

The concepts of human rights and equal opportunities are becoming dominant in our 21st century world. Most certainly we must protect the interests of those with disabilities and those who are most vulnerable to the abuse of power. However the concept of rights for all also implies that there are duties and responsibilities. That may seem obvious. Nevertheless it is paradoxical that at the same time as society accepts the necessity of responsibility and accountability, there is a growing belief that our genetic make-up, and/or our physical environment, control our behaviour. In the debate between nurture and nature it is assumed that one or both of these will be able to account for our actions. Human choice and the responsibilities such choices bring seem to have been forgotten. Surely Lord Hailsham is right when he says:

> [mankind] is the possessor of free will, that is, he really can, within limits, originate new action, and is thus a *first cause*.[1] (Emphasis added.)

---

[1] *The Door Wherein I Went*, p.64.

Freedom and order

We all want to live in an orderly but free and open society. The combination of order and freedom finds its most basic expression in a good family. However, while a good family is not motivated by either equality or rights, the qualities of love, respect, forgiveness and tolerance of differences are best learnt in the context of a stable family. It is highly significant that in the Christian religion we are taught to address God with the family word 'Father' and not the word 'dictator'.

Even science's examination of the fundamental constituents of the natural world in quantum mechanics reveals both a trustworthy order and a genuine freedom. This marvellous and very subtle balance between reliability and openness challenges both pagan/new age mythology's belief in a chaotic world and the deterministic world of the theories of a few physical scientists and many social scientists. Even certain religious teachings imply that God is a great dictator or puppeteer.[2]

---

[2] Some religious people think that their teaching that God rigidly controls all things gives him maximum glory. The biblical teaching is the opposite. The glory of God is seen in his deliberate and willing *submission* to wilful human sin, so that bearing it in the body of Christ, he might bring salvation and forgiveness to sinners.

Freedom and the propagation of evil

All decent people agree that governments and all who hold power over others should respect the dignity of individual human lives. There should be no arbitrary arrest and imprisonment; no torture; no genocide; and no persecution on the grounds of peaceful political or religious beliefs. Individuals and groups should be allowed freedom of speech to campaign for non-violent political and religious causes, as long as the causes for which they contend are not the propagation of evil and, in the long term, harmful to humanity.

A pertinent question

But how does one know whether a particular cause will or will not have harmful effects in the short, medium and long terms? Unless we know what is the source of goodness and human dignity there will be no way of deciding what is good or bad for us. Even the belief that human life has value will not have a rational basis. We will be lost in a sea of relativism where, inevitably, the strong will gain control over the weak and so destroy the very ideals which the concept of 'human rights' was meant to protect and enhance. Unless the concept itself is grounded in a 'morality which transcends the right', human rights will eventually become human desires and the concept will be powerless to protect the weak against the desires of the strong. Even Samuel Rutherford, writing 350 years ago, argued that future generations ('an innocent posterity not yet born'[3]) could be seriously disadvantaged by the unjust domination of the strong of a previous generation.

Consequences of sexual preferences

One obvious example is our sexual behaviour and the way we might propagate the acceptability of its practice in the community. Independent studies[4] have shown what should be fairly obvious, namely that alternatives to conventional marriage are likely to have very harmful effects on children and the following generations—this in spite of the imperfections of marriage we see all around us. In such alternative contexts for sexual expression children are more likely to grow up with a propensity for drug addiction and crime whatever financial benefit they may receive from the state. What we are seeing as the 'right' of adults (the strong) to practise and promulgate their sexual preferences is done at the expense of the emotional and moral well-being of enormous numbers of children (the weak). What about the rights of succeeding generations?

---

[3] *Lex Rex*, p.48f.
[4] For example, Patricia Morgan, *Marriage-Lite: The Rise of Cohabitation and its Consequences* and also *Experiments in Living: The Fatherless Family*, by Rebecca O'Neill.

Subjective morality

However, a society that rejects any knowable transcendental reality also has to believe that there is no Goodness beyond us impinging upon us. In that case, all morality is subjective. It is the invention of individuals or societies or the result of evolutionary processes. A.J. Ayer tells us that his fellow atheist Bertrand Russell held that ethical questions are questions about what people desire and how they may attain it. Although this was his position, Ayer tells us that Russell was discontented with it.[5] Suppose a person desires to be cruel—how can we persuade him that cruelty is wrong? There is no higher standard to which to appeal. After all there have been times in history when the majority in a society approved of cruel behaviour, as for example in Roman times when public entertainment consisted in watching gladiators killing each other. Did that make it right? Almost all of us would say 'no'.

Russell versus Nietzsche
Yet, however reluctantly, atheists have to hold that ethics are entirely subjective. For them there is no alternative. Russell imagines an argument between Buddha and Jesus on the one hand and Nietzsche on the other. The former favour loving even our enemies. Nietzsche would be bored by such a world.

---

[5] *The Concise Encyclopædia of Western Philosophy and Philosophers*, p.285.

He favours a world where men conquer and show great skill in killing. Russell favours Buddha and Jesus but knows no way to prove them right by any argument. He confesses that all he can do is appeal to his own emotions.[6] However it could be countered that Nietzsche too is basing his view on his emotions. If all we have to go on is our emotions, how do we decide which emotions should be followed? Writing in 1960, Russell expresses this conundrum thus:

> I cannot see how to refute arguments for the subjectivity of moral values, but I find myself incapable of believing that all that is wrong with wanton cruelty is that I don't like it.[7]

We may further ask: are not even our own desires contradictory and fleeting? Can we really trust them? What about competing desires between different people?

Is 'rights' the correct word?

Even if it is believed that the concept of 'rights' is grounded in a Goodness that transcends our human ideals, 'rights' is still not the correct word to describe God-given human dignity and worth. Indeed there is a real danger that 'rights' language corrupts the human relationships that are integral to the self-

---

[6] *History of Western Philosophy*, pp.738-9.
[7] Quoted by Mary Warnock in her article, 'Foundations of Morality'.

6

respect of a truly human life. Our humanity is found in the deeply personal relations we have with one another. 'Rights' talk tends to isolate us from one another and so de-personalize our relations, diminishing the very humanity it is supposed to protect.

A reasonable alternative

It would be foolish to attempt to prove the Christian message by human reasoning. However there are some things we can quite properly say. It certainly is reasonable to believe that the One who is the source of the wonder and beauty of the natural world cannot be less than we are. All of us are personal beings and most of us know something (however imperfectly) of the meaning of love.

It would seem reasonable to think that the One who is greater than us, must at least be personal and be possessed of very great love. Love is self-giving and self-sacrificial even to the undeserving. Thus in the cross of Christ, Christians believe God has come to us and taken our sins and sufferings to himself, thus making sense of the human experience of astounding wisdom, beauty and goodness on the one hand and the enormous reality of foolishness, ugliness and evil on the other.

In Christian belief it is God himself who so loves the world that he gives up his divine right so that we are enabled to have the right to be called children of God (see John 1:11-12; 3:16; Phil. 2:5-9). However, this 'right' is not something that can be described in terms of a list of other rights.

Love not legalism
Even though being a child of God has its obligations, these cannot be described merely by a list of rules. Christian obedience to God is not primarily submission to the will of a distant dictator. It is rather an obedience which flows freely from a relationship of deep personal love for God who has made himself known as Saviour and Father. So rather than each claiming his/her rights, we should recognize our duty to love one another. As we have noted, love is self-sacrificial. To exercise love for someone usually will mean giving up some of my supposed rights to help another more fully to realize his/her humanity.

Order, freedom and mutual respect
Even though, in this imperfect world, laws and commandments are needed and are given by God to be obeyed, they do not provide the basis of Christian obedience to God. A good father, while placing certain limitations on his children's behaviour, allows them as much freedom as he can. Thus in the Bible we discover that God's people are called to live as his children in a relationship of trust with him. This is very different from submitting to the will of a remote and unknowable God. If we believe that the

fundamental reality behind the cosmos is 'Father' rather than 'dictator', it will probably affect how we treat others who are under our authority. We will more likely develop societies that balance order with freedom and mutual respect. Tolerance of differences and democracy are more likely to flourish where such a religion predominates.

CHAPTER TWO

THE CASE FOR THE EXISTENCE OF A REAL MORALITY'
C.S. LEWIS'S ARGUMENT

In the first part of C.S. Lewis's *Mere Christianity*, he makes the case for the existence of a Real Morality that transcends our humanity and the physical world—a Real Morality that impinges upon us, making us aware that good and evil really exist. He is arguing that when we say something is good or evil we are not merely talking about our opinions or preferences or those of our society or the survival strategies of our genes (as if genes were intelligent, purposeful agents capable of devising strategies!). Rather are we talking about good and evil as realities in themselves—realities that are not open to examination by the physical sciences. Assuming he is right, that must mean that realities exist that are not in themselves physical. It follows therefore that there is more to reality than the physical world. This conviction lies behind the claims of religion. Here, together with some additions from me, is a summary of his two main points.

Quarrelling, evolutionary biology and social convention

We have heard people quarrelling. They say things such as, 'How'd you like it if...?' or, 'That's my seat—I was in it first' or, 'Give me a bit of your chocolate, I gave you some of mine' or, 'Come on you promised....'

People who say these things are not just saying they don't like the other's behaviour—rather are they appealing to a higher standard which they expect the other person to know about. The other person seldom, if ever, replies: 'But I don't believe in fairness, or kindness or keeping promises' or, 'I don't believe in any standards of behaviour.' Rather, he will try to say that there are particular reasons why he did what he did; or, there is some other reason why he should have that seat; or, things were quite different when he was given the chocolate; or, something else has turned up to prevent him keeping the promise. Quarrelling shows that we try to demonstrate that the other person is in the wrong: he/she has offended against what is right.

A cross-cultural awareness of right and wrong
This conviction that some things are right and others wrong is universal in the human race. Although cultures differ, almost all societies regard such things as fairness, honesty, kindness and courage as good in themselves. This does not mean, of course, that there are not some people who are completely oblivious to

the difference between right and wrong—after all some people are colour blind and can't tell green from blue.

There have been, and are, moral differences between cultures, but the differences are not about whether kindness, fairness, generosity, honesty etc. are good or evil, but how these should be applied and whether they should be applied to all or just to a privileged group.

Here is a quotation from the Bible, which says something similar:

> Indeed, when Gentiles, who do not have the law, [i.e. The Ten Commandments etc.] do by nature things required by the law, they are a law for themselves, even though they do not have the law, since they show that the requirements of the law are written on their hearts, their consciences also bearing witness, and their thoughts now accusing, now even defending them (Rom. 2:14-15, NIV).

Where did this conviction that there exists a Real Morality come from? Either it comes from the physical world: (a) our sense of right and wrong is an instinct that has come from our biological make-up or psychology—which are the results of random evolutionary processes or, (b) our sense of right and wrong comes from social conventions we have learnt or, (c) it is a combination of (a) and (b). Or secondly it comes from beyond the physical world—a spiritual world or God.

Even if the first alternative is part of the story, can it be the whole story? Can explanations from the physical world be right?

The first explanation postulates that our psychology—the result of random evolutionary processes—has led us to value kindness and selflessness. But does not that mean morality is only the instinct to preserve the species? (Note that if the sense of Goodness were just an instinct, which is the result of 'survival of the fittest', then it would have no intrinsic value.)

Two contrary instincts

If we hear of someone in danger there will be two contradictory instincts. There will be the herd instinct to help him, that is, to preserve the species. There will also be the instinct to avoid danger, likewise to preserve the species. However, we will also feel inside us a third impulse which tells us we ought to suppress one instinct and encourage the other. There are appropriate times for each instinct. But morality tells us that at this time that one particular instinct should be given precedence over another. Therefore morality is not itself just a physical instinct.

Leaving C.S. Lewis's argument for a moment, let us note something said by Richard Dawkins (atheist biologist) in his book, *The Selfish Gene*:

> I shall argue that a predominant quality to be expected in a successful gene is ruthless selfishness.... Be warned that if you wish, as I do, to build a society in which

individuals co-operate generously and unselfishly towards a common good, you can expect little help from biological nature. Let us try to teach generosity and altruism, because we are born selfish.[1]

Richard Dawkins does not seem to realize that his desire that we be taught to be unselfish—against our biology—implies that there is purpose to human existence and that something has gone wrong with our human natures which should be countered by purposeful teaching.

Returning to C.S. Lewis, he asks where our moral sense comes from. As we have seen, it does not come from our biology. Has it come then from social conventions which we have learnt? Do we ever think that one social convention is better than another? (One society may believe in slavery while another may not.) Do we think we have progressed, i.e. got better in our moral customs? If we do, then we are implicitly acknowledging another greater Real Morality by which we judge one morality or social convention against another.

An illustration
Suppose two of us had an idea of what New York was like. Your idea might be truer than mine because there is a real place called New York by which we can compare our ideas.

---

[1] *The Selfish Gene*, p.2.

But if we simply meant 'the town I am imagining in my head' (there being no real New York) then one person's idea would be no more correct than the other person's idea. If there were no such thing as Real Morality—but just what evolution made people think, or just what different cultures had developed themselves—there would be no meaning to the statement that Nazi morality is inferior to any other morality.

An 'ought' cannot be derived from an 'is'

Let us turn to a different form of C.S. Lewis's argument that there must be more to morality than can be explained from the physical world. Consider the question: Can one derive an 'ought' from an 'is'?

Science can tell us what *is* the case, but can it tell us what *ought* to be the case? Electrons behave as they do. That is neither morally right nor wrong—it is just the way things are—the whole story. We behave in certain ways but that is not the whole story for we know we ought to behave in certain other ways. Therefore there is more than one kind of reality.

The first of these realities is subject to scientific investigation and discovery; the other one is not. Therefore there must be more than one kind of reality—one physical and the other not. Therefore if our moral sense is neither mere biology/psychology nor social convention and is not open to investigation by physical science, then it must have come from beyond the physical world. That is what religion is about.

This is the basis of C.S. Lewis's argument.

CHAPTER THREE

SCIENTISM, GENETIC DETERMINISM, SOCIOBIOLOGY AND OTHER ILLUSIONS

Scientism

Scientism is the belief that there is nothing in all reality (not even beauty, morality or our sense of freedom) whose explanation cannot be reduced to impersonal atoms, which together with chance have brought about the universe and world of life we have today; there is nothing 'spiritual' which is not amenable to analysis in the laboratory.[1] Scientism can have no evidence to support it. It is a blind faith. (How could it ever be shown that there is nothing

---

[1] The Oxford chemist Peter Atkins is clearly a believer in scientism. He says: 'Science is slowly equipping itself to deal with aesthetic and religious experiences. It will do so, I do not doubt, by showing that these characteristically human capacities... are no more than psychological states of the brain. Likewise, that other component of our existence, the wishful-thinking extension of the idea of "soul" to the expectation of eternal persistence, is already quite plainly explicable in terms of the deep-seated desire to avoid, and the inability to come to terms with, the prospect of one's own annihilation.... I long for immortality, but I know that my only hope of achieving it is through science and medicine, not through sentiment and its subsets, art and theology.' ('The Limitless Power of Science' in *Nature's Imagination*, pp.129-31.)

beyond and behind the world of physics?) The philosopher Professor John Haldane rightly says:

> nothing in the study of nature requires that we only allow as real what physics deals with; to suppose otherwise is a prejudice of philosophy not a discovery of science.[2]

A 'jihad' against belief in God

Putting it another way, physical science examines only physical things. That should be beyond dispute. It clearly follows that physical science cannot provide evidence against the existence of the non-physical. On the contrary it might indicate that physical existence is not the whole story of reality. I believe it does and the case is overwhelming—in whatever direction science makes its probes. I have discussed these in other writings and courses which I teach.[3]

In today's world there is great confusion between the discoveries of science and mathematics, on the one hand, and the 'scientism' which some scientists and others adhere to with a kind of fundamentalist fervour. Their fundamentalism is so strong that they are on a kind of 'jihad' against belief in God.[4]

---

[2] *Atheism and Theism*, p.197.
[3] See outline of *Christianity and Modern Science* at
http://www.apologetics.fsnet.co.uk/courses.htm
[4] An example of this fervour was heard in a lecture, sponsored by Amnesty International, given in Oxford in 1997. The lecturer was Nicholas Humphrey, a psychologist who is part of a closely-knit group of atheist scientists and philosophers which includes Richard Dawkins and Daniel Dennett. The burden of Humphrey's

Is life, and especially our human life with all its experiences of conscious and voluntary decision-making, really just the result of the jostling of atoms whose motions are entirely governed by physical laws? The popular notion about science is that it assumes that all reality can in principle be explained entirely by the laws of physics, chemistry and biology. As noted above, this 'scientism' can never be proved from science itself. However, it is often spoken of as if there was conclusive evidence for it. So philosophical 'materialism' is still widely believed to be the scientific understanding of the way the world is. Some scientists themselves remain materialists in this sense, believing that every event must have a preceding physical cause.

However it should be obvious that what are called 'contra-causal' factors really exist. It simply is not true that human thought, decision and action are the result of the previous distribution of particles in the universe.[5] That is to say that a human being really can be a 'first cause' initiating new action and thinking. Humans genuinely are responsible to a Goodness that transcends the physical world.

---

lecture was that bringing up children in religious faith was an offence against their rights. It was an offence comparable to genital mutilation or foot-binding. (This example is taken from an article entitled, 'The New Pythagoreans' by Andrew Brown in the summer 1997 edition of *Leading Light*. *Leading Light* was the journal of 'Gospel and Culture'.)

[5] This means that physics and dynamics can never be complete.

Determinism and Sociobiology

If, on the contrary, humanity is simply a complex combination of impersonal atoms and physical laws then our behaviour would simply be the result of the interaction of our physical make-up and the physical laws of our environment—**determinism**.

Drusilla Scott's book *Everyman Revived* (about Michael Polanyi, friend of Einstein and one of the 20th century's most original thinkers in the area of the philosophy of science) bids us compare two quotations:

(a) Bertrand Russell wrote: The problem which Pavlov successfully tackled is that of subjecting to scientific law what has hitherto been called voluntary behaviour.... The more this achievement is studied the more important it is seen to be, and it is on this account that Pavlov must be placed among the most eminent men of our time.[6]

(b) 'Heavily Armed Children Prowling Los Angeles' says a recent headline. The juvenile court judge said about these children, who were brought before him for shooting into crowds of people they did not know, and setting fire to an old woman, 'They show no sense of

---

[6] About 1904, the Russian physiologist, Ivan Pavlov, found that sounding a bell every time a dog was about to be given food eventually caused a reflex flow of saliva, which later persisted even when no food was produced. Elaborations of this habituative type of reflex are regarded by some physiologists and psychologists as an important basis for many behaviours, both voluntary and involuntary.

empathy for their victims. It's almost like they are programmed robots out on the prowl to kill.'[7]

In 1996 Professor Steve Jones discussed the genetic basis of criminality to mark the launch of his book and TV series. This was Janet Daley's comment in the *Daily Telegraph*:[8]

> The most important question raised by Steve Jones's essay is not, 'What makes people bad?' but, 'Can anyone ever be said to be good?' If what Jones suggests is true, that criminal behaviour is largely determined by genetic make-up, then it can be said that most criminals are not fully responsible for their acts. But presumably the particular genes that predispose towards the criminal personality cannot be the only ones that influence behaviour. If genetics is responsible for 'bad' traits, it must account for many good ones as well. The hunt for a hypothetical gene for co-operativeness or generosity may not be so urgent since these characteristics do not present social problems, but anyone taking Jones's line would have to grant that they are likely to exist.

At the end of Janet Daley's article she gives this account of a criminal trial in California:

> Take too, Jones's case of John Baker—the alcoholic lawyer who embezzled his clients' money. Mr Baker had American Indian blood which made him particularly susceptible to alcohol. Because this was taken into account, he was not disbarred from his profession as a result of his crimes.

---

[7] Drusilla Scott, *Everyman Revived: the Common Sense of Michael Polanyi*, p.11.
[8] May 2, 1996.

What is of most significance in the story is that, after this salutary experience, John Baker gave up drinking. In other words, he chose to reform himself: he made a decision to fight his inborn weakness. And that is the essence of what moral behaviour has always been thought to be. Indeed, we generally give most moral credit to someone who must fight to resist evil impulses—who, perhaps, was born with great disadvantages.

Have we freedom to make choices?

Following on from Janet Daley's article we can ask: If genes entirely determine our bad behaviour, do they also determine: our good behaviour; our opinions about what is good and what is bad; the decisions that law makers make; the decisions law enforcers make about other people? (How could we tell that my genes produce better behaviour than your genes? What standard could we use to determine what 'better' means?)

Our question is not: 'Do genes affect our behaviour?'—of course they do! The question is rather: 'Could genes and other physical factors provide the complete explanation of why we behave as we do or is there, in addition, genuine free will?'

Sociobiology takes determinism even further, giving us a purpose in life and death. It is the theory that not only do our genes control our behaviour but we actually exist for the benefit of our genes. [9]

---

[9] Richard Dawkins, *The Selfish Gene*.

David Stove, the Australian philosopher who died in 2003, comments:

> Consider the following representative statements made by leading sociobiologists. Richard Dawkins, easily the best-known spokesman for this movement, writes that 'we are... robot-vehicles blindly programmed to preserve the selfish molecules known as genes', and again that we are 'manipulated to ensure the survival of [our] genes' The same writer also says that 'the fundamental truth [is] that an organism is a tool of DNA'. Again, Dawkins says that 'living organisms exist for the benefit of DNA'. Similarly, E.O. Wilson, an equal or higher socio-biological authority, says that 'the individual organism is only the vehicle [of genes], part of an elaborate device to preserve and spread them.... The organism is only DNA's way of making more DNA....' According to the Christian religion, human beings and all other created things exist for the greater glory of God; according to sociobiology, human beings and all other living things exist for the benefit of their genes. The expression 'their genes' is probably not perfectly orthodox, from the strict sociobiological point of view; being rather too apt to suggest that genes are part of our equipment, whereas (according to sociobiology) we are part of theirs.[10]

There have been criticisms of sociobiology by other atheist academics who say it threatens our motivation to change the world for the better.[11] Of course any

---

[10] This is a quotation from David Stove's article, 'A New Religion', in the *Journal of the Royal Institute of Philosophy*, Vol. 57, no. 260, pp. 233-40.

[11] These are mentioned in a very good article, 'Against Sociobiology' by Tom Bethell (Senior Editor of the *American*

determinist understanding of our humanity would have the same effect.

Morality from science?

Attempts have been made to explain the existence of altruism as being a result of random mutation and natural selection.[12]   However even if such explanations were successful and our sense of morality could, one day, be explained completely by our biological make-up, does that mean that there is no such thing as intrinsic good and intrinsic evil, so that cruelty (say) is not in itself evil—it's just that we don't like it?

Physicist Paul Davies hopes that physical science may help us determine true morality. In the February 2000 edition of *The Times* Higher Educational Supplement, Davies, in an article entitled, 'The Gospel According to Science', argues that we must use science to arrive at moral values. Here is a quotation from the article:

> There is an urgent need to reappraise our concepts of right and wrong and to develop an ethical framework appropriate to the scientific opportunities and challenges of the future. Science may never replace the secure ethical certainties of traditional religion, but it does offer a rational basis for moral choice and a framework for

---

Spectator), pp. 18-24.
[12] An article that gives some ground to this view but believes it finally unsuccessful is 'All in the Genes?' by physics professor Russell Stannard.

understanding human selfishness. The father of sociobiology, Edward O. Wilson, has a vision in which ethics is brought within the scope of systematic scientific inquiry, forming a grand synthesis of science and the humanities for which he has appropriated the term 'consilience'.[13]

Difficulties in Davies

There are definite weaknesses in his article. While acknowledging science cannot completely replace religion, his conviction is that we must turn to science to find moral values. Yet he does not indicate what he means by 'goodness'. Moreover there is an underlying assumption that the survival and future happiness of our species is the final goal of goodness and morality. However, he believes humans commit much evil, as well as good. And if, as he says, we do evil things, why should our survival be a 'good'?

But, we must ask, even if it is the case that morality is about our survival and happiness, does that follow from science? If not from science then from what? He also wonders how science can be used to give us moral values but he cannot give any indication of how this might be possible. The reason he cannot succeed is that science tells us what is the case, not what ought to be the case—and (as we have seen) an 'ought'

---

[13] My criticisms of Edward Wilson's Pulitzer Prize-winning book *Consilience* can be found in my review article in *Philosophia Christi* (Vol. 4, No. 1, 2002). It is also available on my web site: www.howardtaylor.net.

cannot be deduced from an 'is'.

Real objective morality—a helpful illusion?

The biologist and philosopher Michael Ruse takes a different tack from that of Paul Davies. His theory[14] is that there is no real 'good'; it is just a useful illusion that helps preserves our species by making us behave more co-operatively. (But if the 'good' is an illusion how can it be claimed that it is 'good' that we behave co-operatively?) He believes that morality comes from our genes that trick us into thinking that co-operation is objectively 'good'. To quote him:

> In the words of myself and my sometime co-author sociobiologist Edward O. Wilson of Harvard University, 'morality is a collective illusion of humankind, put in place by our genes in order to make us good cooperators'.[15]

If we agree with Ruse that it is good that we have this illusion, we must conclude that it is bad that Ruse has enlightened us and taken away our illusion! He is ably criticized by John Byle.[16] John Byle argues that this theory refutes itself and therefore cannot be true. Here is an excerpt from Byle's article:

> If morality, with its concepts of good/bad and right/wrong, were an illusion, then so, it would seem, is

---

[14] See the Templeton Foundation's *Research News and Opportunities in Science and Theology*, February and May 2001.

[15] *Ibid*. See also Ruse's book, *Evolutionary Naturalism*.

[16] The Templeton Foundation's *Research News and Opportunities in Science and Theology*, September 2001.

the notion of genes tricking us into becoming 'good' cooperators. This notion, conveying value, motivation, and purpose, has strong moral implications, even if the adjective 'good' was perhaps not here intended in a strictly moral sense. Consequently, the alleged purpose for morality—to make us 'good' cooperators—is itself an illusion.

Furthermore, what are we to make of Ruse's numerous references to 'good' and 'bad' science, philosophy and religion? Surely he does not seriously believe that he is communicating mere illusions! Yet, if Ruse believes his statements to have genuine, valuable content, then he must reject his own claim regarding the illusion of morality. Indeed, Ruse certainly writes as if he, at least, is not deceived by his genes. Hence, presumably, morality is not an illusion after all. But in that case, Ruse is still left with the perplexing reductionist problem of how to derive a moral 'ought' or 'good' from a naturalist 'is'.

Ruse is driven to drastic claims such as the above by his professed commitment to ontological and methodological reductionism. These entail that all his beliefs, as well as his sense of personal identity, purpose, and free will, are mere illusions caused by his genes (or brain neurones). At least, that is where he seems to end up in his book *Evolutionary Naturalism*.

However, if all our beliefs are illusionary, then so is the belief that our beliefs are illusions caused by genes. How, then, does Ruse explain and justify his beliefs?

CHAPTER FOUR

A CHRISTIAN LORD CHANCELLOR

Our former Lord Chancellor, Lord Hailsham, writes concerning 'two propositions about the nature of man':

> The first is that he is the possessor of free will, that is, he really can, within limits, originate new action, and is thus a first cause. The second is that the value judgements which he makes, and in particular the value judgements about morality and justice, are not mere emotional noises but have an objective validity about which reasoned argument can turn and which respond to something real rooted in the nature of humanity and in the universe itself. There could be no place for law, nor for the sanctions of law, nor political authority if training a man were not different in principle from training a dog or donkey. No doubt there could be sticks and carrots, and in that sense rewards and punishments. But there could be no appeal to reason, and none to justice. There would be no such thing as justice. It is only in a world in which there is morality, and that morality is binding on rulers and ruled alike that there is any room for a jurisprudence in the true sense of the word. This is the world which is asserted by religious belief, and in particular by the world religions. *It is, I believe, for this reason that any attempt by the politician to drive religion out of his philosophy has always led to one thing, which is man's almost total*

inhumanity to man. In the end the utilitarian and individualistic philosophies of the nineteenth century led to the 'wail of intolerable serfdom' spoken of in Disraeli's novels. I need not say to what the collectivist philosophies of the twentieth century have led....

It is a belief in man as a creature made in God's image, to use the poetic language of the Old Testament, which forms the protection of man from the extremities of indifference or oppression. It is the objective validity of morality as proclaimed by the sages of all nations which explains and justifies the perpetual tension, the endless dialogue, between individuals and minorities on the one hand and the State on the other, between freedom and authority, between liberty and law. In other words it is the free will and the rationality of the individual, the dignity of the individual, in tension with the moral responsibility of the individual which explains and justifies the writings of the political authors, the debates in Parliament, the regulations made by Ministers, the treaties concluded between sovereign communities, the demand for freedom, and the necessity for law which constitute the history of the West, and ultimately of all mankind. The fact that these things are not measurable, calculable, or verifiable explains much, perhaps all, of the argument. But the fact that they remain objective realities proves that the argument is not about nothing. A law which does not appeal to the rational in man is no better than a stick or a carrot applied to a donkey, by whomsoever or whatsoever it is passed.... Law and freedom are, therefore, not enemies but friends, not opposites but co-ordinates in a world in which man is a responsible creature with free will and a reason capable of understanding the difference between good and bad.

Only, I believe, the world religions, of which Christianity is the one I am discussing, provide a rational working hypothesis of what this is all about.[1] (Emphasis added.)

---

[1] *The Door Wherein I Went*, p. 64.

CHAPTER FIVE

OPTIMISTIC HUMANISM AND NIETZSCHE'S PESSIMISTIC NIHILISM

Humanism

Of course modern humanism cannot accept Lord Hailsham's view. Taking some inspiration from Protagoras, the ancient Greek philosopher, who is famous for his words, 'Man is the measure of all of things that are, that they are; and of things that are not, that they are not', humanism puts its faith in humanity. Plato rejected Protagoras's view saying that it would make all rational discussion impossible because rational discussion has to start from some common ground. By 'man' Protagoras had meant each individual person. Plato tried to solve the problem by postulating a transcendent world in which the objects and concepts of this world find their true meaning. Probably not understanding the difficulty that Plato perceived, many humanists today still find encouragement in Protagoras's statement, understanding it to mean that we can't trust any supernatural world to guide us. In fact that was not Protagoras's main point.[1]

Modern humanism is an optimistic form of atheism/agnosticism, which believes we have good reason to have faith in humanity. We will soon see that there are deeply pessimistic forms of atheism, which explicitly reject humanism.

Ancient humanism

We have already noted something of Protagoras. Most ancient Greek philosophers believed that our innate ability to reason, not merely about our surroundings but also about universal concepts abstracted from us, gives humans a definite superiority in the living world.[2]

---

[1] What Protagoras actually meant was that each *individual* human being is the source of his own knowledge about things that exist. He argued that none of us can know what another person perceives. Since we cannot enter into another person's mind and know that he perceives what we perceive, there is no certainty that we have the same experience when we see, hear etc. what others see and hear. As noted in the text above Plato later argued that if this were true no rational discussion would ever be possible because there would be no common standard by which to judge one another's opinions about truth. Plato's solution was to propose a superior world where reality resides—a world that impinges upon our own—so that the 'shadows' of reality that exist in our world are shadows of realities in the 'real world'. In Plato's view it was this real superior world that provides us with the basis for rational discussion.

[2] For example, humans can discuss 'what it is to be a dictatorship' even if they have never experienced or even heard or read of anyone else's experience of a dictatorship. This ability

Everywhere we look in nature we see 'order'. Since order ultimately depends on 'mind', the Greek philosophers concluded that there was a universal mind pervading nature and that human beings alone among all of this world's many creatures share in this universal mind.[3]

Renaissance humanism (15th and 16th centuries)

Renaissance humanism celebrated a freedom of thought that came from less dependence on Christian doctrine. The church's teaching no longer provided the unshakeable foundation for true thought.

Although knowledge became less dependent upon the church, underpinning this humanism was faith in the goodness of the natural world—a goodness derived from its good Creator. Right and wrong could be discerned from 'the way the world is' or 'natural law'. For example, John Locke in the post-Renaissance 17th century based his belief in 'human rights' on 'natural law' which was ultimately

---

to discuss abstract universal concepts with which one has never had any physical interaction is a powerful argument against materialism/physicalism.

[3] They had no belief in a creator or creation (although Aristotle believed in a Prime Mover), so nature has to be as it is by logical necessity. Therefore they believed reason, logic and mathematics alone—*without the need for experimentation*—could be used to unlock the mysteries of the universe. This is the most probable reason why experimental science never really took off in the otherwise brilliant ancient Greek world.

dependent upon the existence of a good God.[4]
Bertrand Russell comments:

> The view of the state of nature and of natural law which
> Locke accepted from his predecessors cannot be freed
> from its theological basis; where it survives without
> this, as in much modern liberalism, it is destitute of
> clear logical foundation.[5]

Another problem for the theory of natural law is that
many people (not just Christians) believe the world is
not the way it ought to be. Thus Christians at least
should believe that our concept of right and wrong
must come from the nature of God himself revealed
in the gospel which renews God's creation. It cannot
come just from creation as it is now and the way the
world is now.

Post-Enlightenment and modern atheistic humanism
After Newton's discoveries of the 'laws of motion'
governing the movement of bodies (large and small),
many gradually came to believe that eventually all
things would be explicable by physical laws alone.
Implicit in this belief was the assumption that the
laws of nature (such as gravity) were eternal.[6]   So

---

[4] David Hume (18th century) discounted the concept of 'rights'
because it could not be empirically verified and therefore
belonged to metaphysics, which he rejected.
[5] *History of Western Philosophy*, p.602.
[6] Although this understanding of the laws of nature has been
outdated for nearly a century, it is still a popular misconception
about the scientific worldview.

now there had developed a growth of humanism without a belief in God.

This inevitably led to a belief in a mechanistic universe, which itself would reduce humans to mere complex mechanisms and rob them of a basic and inherent personality. It is this that drives the honest thinking atheist to the deep pessimism found in some forms of existentialism and especially the nihilism of Nietzsche (as we will see). Nevertheless modern humanism maintains its optimistic belief in the goodness of humanity.

The following are excerpts from the British Humanist Association's declaration of its main convictions:

- humanists reject the idea of any supernatural agency intervening to help or hinder us
- evidence shows that we have only one life, and humanists grasp the opportunity to live it to the full
- humanists retain faith… that people can and will continue to solve problems, and that quality of life can be improved and made more equitable
- humanists are positive, gaining inspiration from a rich natural world, our lives and culture
- humanists think that
  - this world and this life are all we have

- we should try to live full and happy lives ourselves and, as part of this, make it easier for other people to do the same

- all situations and people deserve to be judged on their merits by standards of reason and humanity

- individuality and social co-operation are equally important.[7]

Underlying these bold and optimistic statements is the conviction that humanity (not God) is the correct object of faith. We should do what is natural because we are basically good. How then is goodness measured? By our feelings as to the difference between right and wrong? But our feelings are often contradictory. If Hitler had won the war and then brainwashed everyone to believe that genocide was good, that would not have made it good.

To be happy, we must be happy
Also underlying modern humanism's convictions is the belief that we must promote human happiness. No sane person would quarrel with that. However, how do we know what is good for the promotion of human happiness in the long term? Human happiness comes from a sense of purpose which is being fulfilled. What is this purpose? Is humanity's purpose in life to be happy? If that is the case, all that

---

[7] Taken from the British Humanist Association's web site.

is being said is that in order for humanity to be happy it must be happy!

Another underlying belief of contemporary humanism is that reason and freedom are other essential aspects of our humanity. However, if we are nothing but bundles of matter and physical laws, can there be real freedom or even effective reasoning?[8]

Nietzsche's nihilistic atheism

This leads us back to Nietzsche. Here is just one among many examples of his rejection of objective morality:

> Who can attain to anything great if he does not feel in himself the force and will to inflict great pain? The ability to suffer is a small matter: in that line, weak women and even slaves often maintain masterliness. But not to perish from internal distress and doubt when one inflicts great suffering and hears the cry to it—that is great, that belongs to greatness.[9]

Although he lived over a hundred years ago his influence is still strong to this day. The extreme left, the extreme right and the extreme liberal often look to him for inspiration. In the book, *After Progress*, the philosopher Anthony O'Hear notes the strange craze among so-called liberals for Nietzsche, the

---

[8] Reasoning is only possible when there is freedom for thought. A mechanistic view of humanity would remove any freedom.

[9] Friedrich Nietzsche, *The Joyful Wisdom*, trans. by Thomas Common, New York, 1964, p.25.

philosophical precursor of fascism, from whom they have derived the self-deluding idea that morality is merely a device to wield power over others.[10]

Nietzsche's *Thus Spake Zarathustra* begins with pronouncement by Zarathustra that God is dead. Because God is dead (said Nietzsche), it follows that: the physical world with its laws is all that there is; there is no real 'I' independent of my body/brain (see quotation below); there is no such thing as free thought; there is no such thing as reasoning and therefore no real knowledge.

> As for the superstitions of the logicians,[11] I shall never tire of underlining a concise little fact which these superstitious people are loath to admit—namely that a thought comes when it wants, not when 'I' want; so that it is a falsification of the facts to say: the subject 'I' is the condition of the predicate 'think'.[12]

Is it true there is no truth?

It seems as if science as knowledge of the real universe is an illusion and there are no such things as good and evil. In an age of dramatic scientific discoveries we decide that we know nothing. To the obvious question, 'How can it be true that there is no

---

[10] I owe this insight to an article by Melanie Phillips 'Waking to a false dawn of freedom without duty', *The Sunday Times*, January 2, 2000.

[11] By 'logicians' Nietzsche means scientists and others who believe genuine thought is possible. He is saying that 'thinking', as we normally consider it, is not possible.

[12] Nietzsche, *Beyond Good and Evil*, section 17.

truth?' he provides no answer. Nor can he. Nietzsche enjoys the irony that the rationality that made science possible has been destroyed by science. There is no objective purpose to life, neither good nor evil. We must now seize the moment, say 'yes' to life, and impose our will on the world around us. We must be strong-willed. Truth is not discovered, it is created. Truth is the will to power.[13]

As we have seen, in order to combat the loss of rationality that he claimed would be the result of Protagoras's view that 'man is the measure of all things', Plato believed in a transcendent world where eternal reality resides. Nietzsche, of course, rejected this.

Consider now a well-known postmodernist thinker, Richard Rorty:

> When contemporary admirers of Plato claim that all featherless bipeds—even the stupid and childlike, even the women, even the sodomized—have the same inalienable rights, admirers of Nietzsche reply that *the very idea of inalienable human rights* is, like the idea of a special added ingredient, *a laughably feeble attempt by the weaker members of the species to fend off the stronger.*

> As I see it, one important intellectual advance made in our century is the steady decline of interest in the quarrel between Plato and Nietzsche. There is a growing willingness to neglect the question, 'What is our nature?' and to substitute the question, 'What can

---

[13] I owe this insight into Nietzsche to Ian Markham's *Truth and the Reality of God* (T&T Clark, Edinburgh, 1998).

we make of ourselves?'... We are coming to think of ourselves as the flexible, protean, self-shaping animal rather than as the rational animal or the cruel animal.

One of the shapes we have recently assumed is that of a *human rights culture*.... We should stop trying to get behind or beneath this fact, stop trying to detect and defend its so-called 'philosophical presuppositions'.... Philosophers like myself... *see our task as a matter of making our own culture—the human rights culture—more self-conscious and more powerful, rather than of demonstrating its superiority to other cultures* by an appeal to something trans-cultural.[14] (Emphases added.)

But if there is no rational basis for an understanding of human nature, why should we engage in the 'task as a matter of making our own culture—the human rights culture—more self-conscious and more powerful'? There simply is no answer to that. Neither Plato nor Nietzsche would be satisfied with Rorty's exhortation. It does not engage the argument. It avoids it.

This brings us near to the issue of human rights itself. But first we must consider a little more closely the nature of Real Goodness.

---

[14] Richard Rorty, *Human Rights, Rationality and Sentimentality*. Richard Rorty is Professor of Comparative Literature in the USA and a well-known supporter of postmodernism.

CHAPTER SIX

GOODNESS—REAL BUT BEYOND PRECISE DEFINITION

I believe we have established that Goodness is real and that its origin and source is outside the physical world but that nevertheless it pervades all things. In other words our moral awareness that some things are 'right' and other things are 'wrong' comes from a Real Goodness that is above and beyond us—pressing upon us. It is not just our society's subjective judgement that, for example, 'human life is valuable'. Such a judgement cannot merely be just a good survival strategy for our genes to make us believe that human life is precious.

Rather, human life is intrinsically valuable because God our Father greatly values it. (The fatherhood rather than the dictatorship of God is important here.) When we say: 'cruelty is wrong' or 'kindness is good', we are not merely speaking about our own feelings or culture (individual or collective), but about a morality real in itself—rooted in the love and the purpose of God for our human lives. In that loving purpose, God has given us commandments. However, the source of our sense of goodness is not a list of 'Moral Laws' coming from beyond us.

Beauty

We turn for a moment to think of beauty. Even though we may be able, for example, to think of certain attributes that could help us describe the beauty of a mountain scene, beauty or grandeur cannot be defined by a list of attributes. Beauty is a reality that transcends formal definition. However it doesn't follow that it is imaginary or entirely subjective.

Similarly, when we say, 'The valley is beautiful', we are not merely talking about our own feelings. We are claiming that beauty is something that is actually there. Although our subjective feelings have an important role in the appreciation of beauty they cannot be the whole story. It simply is not true that it is a purely subjective judgement that Mozart's symphonies are more beautiful than the sound of a pneumatic drill. If there really is no intrinsic difference between the two sounds we would have to say with Lord Hailsham:

> [There would be no] reason why all human experiences of the same subject matter should be given an equal value, the saint's insights made no better than those of the criminal's, the philistine's equated with the aesthete's, that of the tone-deaf lumped with the musician, even though, unlike the judgements of science, they be incapable of verification.[1]

---

[1] *The Door Wherein I Went*, p.13.

Could a person captivated by a beauty he is experiencing at the same moment be planning evil? It would be difficult (though not impossible[2]) to imagine that normally this could be so. In the Psalms we often read of the psalmist speaking or singing of the grandeur of the natural world and at the same time singing of the righteousness of God. It would seem then that beauty and grandeur are connected with goodness, which is also something real. It is the biblical conviction that ugliness, evil and suffering are alien intrusions. Beauty is objectively real, but it is not definable by a list of qualities.

Goodness beyond precise definition

Similarly, I believe, goodness transcends our ability to define it. This is because it is deeply personal and one cannot fully describe a personality in words alone. Words may be helpful but the full appreciation of that personality can only come by living in the presence of that person and engaging in conversation in a relaxed atmosphere of genuine friendship.

The biblical message is focused in the Person of Jesus in whom God meets us face to face and self-sacrificially suffers for our sins, thereby giving us forgiveness, lifting us up in his resurrection and ascension to where we belong eternally. For

---

[2] It is well known, however, that Hitler's Gestapo enjoyed listening to classical music.

Christians, that is the meaning of 'love' and it sums up true goodness. The whole Bible testifies to this love in the belief that God really does divinely empathize with broken humanity and is able finally to forgive and heal us. The process goes on in the entire world but is seen in special intensity in his chosen people Israel.[3] God's struggle with them and their struggle with him is at the heart of human history from Abraham to the end of the world. In the midst of this history (which still today testifies to the truth of the Bible story) comes the One who sums up in himself the meaning of God's dealing with Israel and the wider world.

We are called to be godly—that is to say we should love as God loves us. From this comes our duties of respect for justice and the dignity of our fellow human beings and all creation.

Goodness as the light and love of Christ
However, in our yet imperfect world God knows we still need laws so, by his grace, he gives to us the Ten Commandments and the application of them by Jesus.[4] Even if we don't recognize it at first, the light of the Spirit and Word of God (the source of creation,

---

[3] The name 'Israel' means 'the one with whom God struggles' or 'the one who struggles with God'. The derivation of the word is found in the haunting story recounted in Genesis 32:22-30 but its full meaning is found throughout Israel's long and unique story—a story that reaches out to the end of time.

[4] As, for example, in the Sermon on the Mount (Matt. 5).

beauty and goodness), shines through all creation, impinging upon us all. So we come to recognize righteousness and evil for what they are. That Goodness is not just the goodness of the natural world but derives from the love and light of Christ who is the source both of creation and the redemption of the world. By the grace of God the light of Christ shines (however dimly) on even those who have not heard the details of his great love for humanity and all creation. This is what undergirds all creation and gives all humanity its conviction that Goodness is real and that self-sacrifice, humility and courage are worthwhile. The New Testament expresses it in these words:

> The true light that gives light to every man was coming into the world (John 1:9, NIV).

CHAPTER SEVEN

NATIONAL GOVERNMENTS SUBJECT TO THE EUROPEAN COURT OF HUMAN RIGHTS

As we have seen, when someone says of certain government actions or legislation that it is just or unjust, they are implicitly appealing to a sense that there is a real Justice which he/she expects us to recognize—a Justice by which they expect governments to judge the difference between right and wrong action. Bertrand Russell acknowledges this but adds that without a belief in God and the Bible the way of distinguishing between good and bad laws becomes more difficult.[1] As an atheist he offers no solution—indeed, he cannot.

Governments and the source of justice

Traditional

Our traditional belief is that the goodness of God and his commandments provided society with an appreciation of the difference between right and wrong. This is still signified in the coronation of the sovereign by the Christian church in the name of Christ. The laws of the state as far as possible are

---

[1] *History of Western Philosophy*, p. 605.

meant to be in harmony with that goodness and law of God. State legislation does give certain rights in certain contexts—for example the 'right' of way at a crossroads. But such a 'right' is not a fundamental human right. In a dim way, governments realize that there has to be some objective standard by which they make judgements about right and wrong legislation.

Human rights legislation

I am not claiming that the modern concept of human rights was or is being driven by sinister motives. I believe that in a hazy way it is recognized that moral relativism cannot work and that some kind of 'faith' is needed to sustain the moral fabric of society. In his essay, 'The Spirit of the Laws, the Laws of the Spirit', John Witte says:

> The modern human rights movement was thus born out of desperation…. It was an attempt to find a world faith to fill a spiritual void. It was an attempt to harvest from the traditions of Christianity and the Enlightenment the rudimentary elements of a new faith and a new law that would unite a badly broken world order.[2]

A new 'god'

With the declining influence of the churches and the growth of religious fanaticism, society desperately needs to find a new 'god' in which to anchor a

---

[2] John Witte, Jr, 'The Spirit of the Laws, the Laws of the Spirit'.

morality that can hold society together. Where there is conflict between the European Court of Human Rights and government legislation, human rights, as interpreted by this European Court has the final say.[3] As in a religion, people are reluctant to challenge a new 'god'.

However this has its inevitable problems. As the Encyclopaedia Britannica comments:

> Some of the most basic questions have yet to receive conclusive answers. Whether human rights are to be validated by intuition, custom, social contract theory; whether they are to be understood as irrevocable or partially revocable; whether they are to be broad or limited in number and content—these and kindred issues are matters of ongoing debate and likely will remain so as long as there exist contending approaches to public order and scarcities among resources.

We must now proceed to ask how all this began in the modern era.

American Declaration of Independence

The eighteenth-century Declaration of Independence proclaimed by the thirteen American Colonies on July 4, 1776, stated:

> We hold these truths to be *self-evident*, that all men are *created equal*, that they are *endowed by their Creator* with certain inalienable *Rights*, that among these are Life, Liberty and the Pursuit of Happiness. (Emphases added.)

---

[3] This is so unless Britain actually leaves the EU.

Utilitarianism

This statement about the individual's rights has properly inspired many. It is great rhetoric. Nevertheless it is more than rhetoric. At the time of writing this booklet, its meaning is being contested in the American courts as they decide whether or not an Alabama courthouse should be allowed to have the Ten Commandments displayed on its main entrance.[4]

However, as well as its good points, the Declaration has its problems. First, we need to ask whether its claim really is 'self-evident'? For example, Karl Marx believed that the whole class was all-important and not each individual within it. To quote Bertrand Russell:

> In its absolute form, the doctrine that an individual has certain inalienable rights is incompatible with utilitarianism, i.e. with the doctrine that right acts are those that do most to promote the general happiness.[5]

It was for this reason that Jeremy Bentham, the founder of utilitarianism, characterized the 'rights of man' as 'nonsense'.[6]

---

[4] Those who want the display removed argue that the American Constitution separates church and state. Those in favour of its retention quote this declaration to show that the separation of state and church does not mean the separation of state and God.

[5] *History of Western Philosophy*, p.606.

[6] *Ibid.*, p.695

Second, many have explicitly denied the existence of a Creator and therefore, to them, 'created equal' could not make any sense. For example atheistic Darwinism presents its believers with a conundrum. Bertrand Russell again:

> If men developed by such slow stages that there were creatures which we should not know whether to classify as human or not, the question arises: at what stage in evolution did men, or their semi-human ancestors begin to be all equal?... A resolute egalitarian... will be forced to regard apes as equals of human beings. And why stop with apes? I do not see how he is to resist arguments in favour of Votes for Oysters.[7]

Third, what does 'equal' mean? Am I due equal honour as my parents, children, teachers and students? In some senses 'yes' but not in all senses, as the honour due to parents is self-evidently somewhat different to the honour due to children and the honour due to teachers is not the same as that due to their students.

Fourth, can I find 'happiness' by pursuing it or is it a by-product of something else I pursue?

An acknowledgement of God
On the positive side we can be grateful for the reference to 'created' and 'Creator'. It is not governments who give us our human worth but God. So Thomas Jefferson, America's third

---

[7] *Ibid.*, p.697–8.

President, asserted that his countrymen were a 'free people claiming their rights as derived from the laws of nature and not as the gift of their Chief Magistrate'. By 'Chief Magistrate' he meant government. Nevertheless the problem of the word 'rights' still remains. We return to that shortly.

A long time has passed since Thomas Jefferson; since then a major change has taken place in our understanding of 'rights'. It is now held that they are no longer derived from the Creator but are absolute in themselves. To quote Oliver O'Donovan:[8]

> What is distinctive about the modern conception of rights, however, is that subjective rights *are taken to be original, not derived*.[9] (Emphasis added.)

In other words, contrary to what the founding fathers believed, 'rights' are perceived as not being derived from God, nor indeed from government or anything else. The contemporary assumption is that they can somehow be discovered within us. However, if this is the case there is no way to stop these rights simply becoming our wishes. Since we have competing desires the dominant will inevitably impose their will on others. For example, in a media-dominated age, the desires of those having most control in the media will shape the minds of whole societies. Eventually parliaments will pass laws and

---

[8] Regius professor of Moral and Pastoral Theology, University of Oxford.
[9] *The Desire of the Nations*

repeal others, subverting the humanity of the vulnerable. Is this not what is happening already?[10] Albeit, note that it is always done at first in the name of 'rights' and 'equality'. Inevitably dilemmas which arise have been addressed in newspaper articles.[11]

Specifically addressing the problems caused by human rights legislation, *The Sunday Times* published an article entitled, 'Cleaning up in court: the flood of legal action set to engulf Britain'.[12] Here are some excerpts:

> The largest number of claims brought under the Human Rights Act will involve criminal cases where defendants believe they have been denied a fair trial.... The Football Supporters Association is considering suing the Belgian authorities on behalf of hundreds of England fans who were arrested and deported from Euro 2000 without a court hearing.... Seizing the fortunes of crime barons on suspicion that they have been amassed through organized crime, such as drug smuggling and human trafficking, could also be challenged. A successful challenge will scupper

---

[10] Among other things, I am thinking of the media-inspired subversion of marriage—a God-given relationship which acts as a restraint on our sexual desires. As academic studies have shown very convincingly, diminishing this restraint seriously damages children—the really vulnerable in society. For example see *Marriage-Lite*, by Patricia Morgan.

[11] For example, see article by Annabel Miller, 'Is fundamentalism in danger of becoming a blanket word for the general repression of human rights?', *The Times*, August 29, 1998.

[12] *The Sunday Times*, August 6, 2000.

proposed police efforts to target 39 underworld figures who have amassed fortunes totalling £220m.

Past precedents of rulings using Article 6 include:

Robert Thompson and Jon Venables, the child killers of toddler James Bulger, were awarded £43,000 in costs and damages by the European Court in Strasbourg after it ruled that it was wrong for them to have been tried in an adult court, as they could not have understood the proceedings, and for a politician—in this case Michael Howard, then home secretary—to decide on their final sentence.... The 'M25 gang', the trio of black men jailed for a spree of robbery and murder, was freed last month after it emerged that police had paid an informant £10,000 to give evidence at their trial and public interest immunity certificates had been used to deny the defense team this information. After a ruling at Strasbourg in February that this had impeded their right to a fair trial, the Court of Appeal freed them although the judge did not declare them innocent.

In *The Times*, the late Cardinal Basil Hume, explained how the rights movement needs a moral foundation:

It is not the State or society which confers... rights. So where do they come from? First, both rights and duties flow from the innate value and dignity of every human life, and from the fact that we share a common humanity. *Secondly, if claims to human rights are genuinely to serve human well-being, to be more than exercises in mere self-assertion, they need a secure moral foundation....* We need to embrace a vision of human fulfilment in which we accept that each person is another 'self' and that your rights are my responsibility. I believe that religion underpins the claims of human rights, even if the record of religions is not unblemished. For Christians and

Jews, we are each made in the image and likeness of God.[13] (Emphases added.)

Although I agree with Basil Hume, I believe a Christian account of goodness must go beyond the statement that we are made in the 'image of God'. That wonderful phrase needs to be unpacked. Its full meaning, I believe, is seen in the humanity of Jesus and the gospel itself. We will return to this later.

Newbigin's criticism of the human rights concept

Right to life, liberty and pursuit of happiness

In *Foolishness to the Greeks*,[14] Lesslie Newbigin considers the expression of rights in the American Declaration. He asks us to consider what is true happiness. If we can't ask the question, 'What is the chief purpose of man's existence?', then happiness is whatever each person defines it as. Without belief in heaven or hell, the pursuit of happiness is carried out in the few uncertain years before death, and for many it will become an evermore hectic and anxiety-filled search. If everyone claims the right to life, liberty and happiness, who is under obligation to honour this claim? In the Middle Ages there were reciprocal rights and duties. One could not exist without the other and all were finite.

---

[13] 'A Life Less Arbitrary', *The Times*, December 10, 1998.
[14] This summary is from pp. 26-7 and 118ff.

Replacing God by the state

But since the quest for happiness is infinite, who has the infinite duty to honour the infinite claims? The answer is perceived to be the nation state. However the demands on the state are without limit and inevitably we look to the nation state to replace God as the source to which we look for happiness.

Wants or needs? Right- or left-wing?

In very general terms, British right-wing governments have wanted to give priority to a person's wants over public service provision for what the state believes are their needs. It follows that their policies have emphasized low taxation and low public spending. British left-wing governments have wanted to provide services for what they decide are people's needs. Thus 'tax and spend' has been the policy of left-leaning governments.[15] The argument of the left assumes that need creates a right that has priority over the wants of those who wish to pursue personal happiness in the way they choose.

Two difficulties

The first concerns my wants. My wants may be (and often are) irrational. I can (and often do) want things that would not in the end bring me lasting

---

[15] There is an economic fallacy behind this desire to spend more on public services. It is the fallacy that higher taxation will lead to more money in government coffers. However taxation set at too high a level depresses the economy and actually leads to less money for the government to spend.

happiness. My real needs, what I need to reach my true end, may be different from the wants I feel.

The second concerns my needs. Governments can only give needs priority over wants if there is some socially accepted view of the goal of human existence. But there cannot be a socially accepted priority for needs over wants unless there is a socially accepted doctrine of what human needs really are—in other words, a socially accepted doctrine of the nature and destiny of the human being. Such a socially accepted doctrine is excluded by the dogma of pluralism that controls post-Enlightenment society.

A possible abuse of state power
This latter criticism by Newbigin is very relevant today. For example, a government may decide that children need to be taught certain views of human sexuality. If governments put their beliefs about our children's needs before what parents think their children need and therefore what parents want for their children, there could be a very serious abuse of state power. By what standard do we make judgements in such cases?

CHAPTER EIGHT

INDIVIDUAL WANTS AND NEEDS OR THE GENERAL GOOD? FREEDOM OR ORDER?

Bonds that hold us together

External bonds

By 'external bonds' is meant those things that may bind us to one another but which are external to what we are in ourselves. For example, I could be tied to another person by a rope. The rope is a third thing holding the two of us together. It is external to what we actually are. Another example is a contract I may make with a builder or an employee. Such a contract is a third thing.

Government legislation holds human communities together but a community cannot be defined, far less created, by mere legislation. Such external links are necessary but cannot provide the basis for human community because they are impersonal and, as with contracts, they are conditional.

Internal bonds

By this is meant something that holds me in relationship with another person and which belongs to what we are in and of ourselves. An example is friendship. Friendship is not a 'third thing' added to us. Friendship comes from what it is to be a person.

If I try to define the friendship I have with another by detailing its duties and obligations, I am more likely to spoil the friendship than strengthen it. That does not mean that friendship does not have its obligations; it does. Nevertheless it does not depend on a list of conditions. Its obligations are beyond precise definition because it is personal and a person cannot be described in terms of a list of rights, desires, attributes and faults. If however the friendship has become sour and there is a desire to restore it, a temporary list of obligations might be helpful.

Marriage and family
A better example might be marriage and the family, which are the deepest forms of unconditional human friendships. If a marriage is near to breaking-point but the desire is to save it, it might be helpful temporarily to separate and with the help of a list of commitments try to engage in reconciliation. However both parties must recognize that a fully reconciled union will not have this list as the basis of its renewed life, because true love cannot be defined in terms of a list of obligations, rights and conditions.

This is why the apostle Paul tells us that the law was added because of transgressions.[1]

God's relationship with us

Does God's relation with us depend on external bonds such as 'works of the law' by which we seek to justify ourselves? Or does it depend on internal personal bonds of a child to a Father? Surely it depends entirely on the latter, for that relationship comes from what God is in himself as God and what we are in ourselves as human beings. In other words our relationship with him is by grace and faith—words which include within their meanings the deeply personal characteristics of love and trust, which again contain within their meanings obligations, but obligations that cannot be precisely defined. It is for this reason that marriage is so basic to the human community.[2]

Some theologians have expressed this difference between works of the law on the one hand and grace

---

[1] 'What, then, was the purpose of the law? It was added because of transgressions until the Seed to whom the promise referred had come' (Gal. 3:19, NIV).

[2] Attempts to make marriage just one among several options for the context of expressing sexual union and rearing children will have the inevitable effect of undermining marriage and with it the whole human community, breaking it apart.

and faith on the other as the difference between contract and covenant.[3]

Pebbles, the Ocean and the Web

I owe the helpful analogy of Pebbles, the Ocean and the Web to Harold Turner's books, *Frames of Mind* and *The Roots of Science*. The analogy will help us to understand a third kind of relationship in addition to the external and internal bonds we have just considered.

Pebbles

This corresponds to what I will call 'external relations'. Imagine pebbles on a beach. They do not belong together except by accident. Each pebble remains a pebble whether or not it is with other pebbles. Touching another pebble does not make it more or less a pebble. The one pebble is not necessarily affected by what happens to many pebbles. It can exist by itself. In this analogy relations are external and incidental.

The human rights movement tends to separate us into self-contained individuals each demanding his/her own rights, without a corresponding concern for the general good.

---

[3] Not all agree that technically this is a correct use of these words. Whether this is true or not, what is being expressed in the thinking behind this proposed distinction is surely right and very important.

The Ocean

This is most similar to Eastern religions' view of reality where we don't have the problem of the relation of the one with the many. Each individual does not exist as a permanent reality. We are all different manifestations of the One and our destiny is to lose our individuality in the one Ocean. In this analogy relations are impermanent and ephemeral. The analogy also relates to the utilitarian and Marxist view of ethics, namely that the good of society as a whole overrides the rights of the individual.

The Web

This corresponds to what I have called 'internal relations'. It is not possible to picture internal relations between one and the many. Not only are they indefinable; they cannot be described by a picture. I believe that this 'unpicturability' is due to our full humanity transcending that four-dimensional world of space-time with which we are familiar. The best we can do is use the term 'web' because each part of the web is what it is in relation to other parts of the web.

Consider the comments of both F.F. Bruce and C.S. Lewis who independently reflect on Paul's frequent references to people being 'in Christ' or 'in Adam'. Explaining the apostle Paul's comparison of Adam with Christ in Romans 5:12-21, Bruce writes:

> Paul was thoroughly conversant with the Hebrew concept of corporate personality, and his thought could

easily oscillate on the one hand between the first man Adam and sinful mankind, and on the other hand between Christ, 'the second Adam', and the community of the redeemed. And very properly so: our solidarity with our fellows is a reality which we tend to overlook in the assertion of our individual independence. 'No man is an island, entire of itself.... Any man's death diminishes me, because I am involved in Mankind; And therefore never send to know for whom the bell tolls: it tolls for thee.' John Donne's oft-quoted words express a permanent truth. Because we live in separate bodies we tend to think that all other aspects of our personality are equally self-contained, but they are not.[4]

C.S. Lewis expresses a very similar perception when commenting on Paul's Adam/Christ comparison in 1 Corinthians 15:22:

We have recently been told by the scientists that we have no right to expect that the real universe should be picturable, and if we make mental pictures to illustrate quantum physics we are moving away from reality, not nearer to it. We have clearly even less right to demand that the highest spiritual realities should be picturable, or even explicable in terms of our abstract thought. I observe that the difficulty on the Pauline formula turns on the word 'in', and that this word, again and again in the New Testament, is used in senses we cannot fully understand. That we can all die 'in' Adam and live 'in' Christ seems to me to imply that man, as he really is, differs a good deal from man as our categories of thought and our three dimensional imaginations represent him; that the separateness—modified only by causal relations— which we discern between

---

[4] *Romans*, pp.126-7.

individuals, is balanced, in absolute reality, by some kind of 'inter-inanimation' of which we have no conception at all. It may be that the acts and sufferings of great archetypal individuals such as Adam and Christ are ours, not by legal fiction, metaphor, or causality, but in some much deeper fashion. There is no question of course of individuals melting down into a kind of spiritual continuum such as Pantheistic systems believe in; that is excluded by the whole tenor of our faith. But there may be a tension between individuality and some other principle.[5]

In this 'web' analogy, relations are internal and constitutive. My real 'self' is constituted, maintained and eternally guaranteed in relations with other selves. Other selves include, not only human beings but of course, God and the higher animals—animals that he created so that humans should not be alone on earth.[6]

The inexplicable interaction of electrons

In fundamental physics, wave-particles such as electrons do not exist as isolated entities, but their very existence comes from relationships.[7] Once two

---

[5] Lewis, C.S., *The Problem of Pain*, pp.74-5.

[6] Genesis 2:18-19.

[7] In the 1930s, it was predicted that once two fundamental wave particles, say electrons, have interacted, then the result of the measurement on one will depend on the result of the measurement on the other, even if they are separated by vast distances, and in nature there is no way in which they can 'communicate' with each other. Experiments using electron spin have verified this result, which is usually called EPR after Einstein, Podolsky and Rosen who first predicted it.

electrons have interacted, their behaviours become interdependent even though they may be separated by millions of miles and there appears to be no way in which they can communicate!

Now it would be very rash to use quantum theory as evidence for Christian doctrine, but it might make it less difficult for us to believe that the one in whom 'all things hold together'[8] can really embrace our humanity and yet preserve our freedom as human beings.

Jesus describes his own coming crucifixion as gathering together all the sin of previous generations.[9] The New Testament speaks of the death of Christ as an actual bearing of all human sin—even the sins of those not actually physically present at his crucifixion. Christians believe this is not a legal fiction but is a spiritual reality. Even though we 21st century Europeans are separated in our humanity from Christ's earthly ministry by two thousand miles and two thousand years, nevertheless we can sing the words of Charles Wesley: 'Died he for me who caused his pain, for me who him to death pursued.'[10] Other hymns also express this sentiment which for Christians is an amazing spiritual and eternal reality.

---

[8] Colossians 1:17.

[9] Matthew 23:31-37.

[10] The hymn's first words are, 'And can it be that I should gain an interest in the Saviour's blood?'

The quantum physicist John Polkinghorne writes:

Jesus may have died for himself; how could he have died for me? If we are all totally separate from each other, living lives of insulated independence, I think it is very hard to see how that question finds an answer. But, however strange it may seem to twentieth-century man to say so, I do not think that the strictly individualistic model is the correct picture of mankind. If there is a deep level at which human solidarity prevails, then it can be the case, as the writer to the Hebrews says, that Jesus is 'the pioneer of our salvation' (Heb. 2:10, RSV), for at that level we are joined to him.[11]

And if joined to Christ, then joined to one another.

The Trinity

It almost goes without saying that the Trinity is the source of these constitutive and eternal relations. This doctrine has often been thought to be dry and divorced from our normal understanding. When we consider that relations beyond our present world are indefinable within the restricted dimensions of our everyday life, and also that our human experience indicates that these dimensions are only part of reality, then we should not be surprised by the following verses from the Bible:

However, as it is written: 'No eye has seen, no ear has heard, no mind has conceived what God has prepared for those who love him'—but God has revealed it to us by his Spirit. The Spirit searches all things, even the deep things of God (1 Cor. 2:9-10, NIV).

---

[11] Polkinghorne, J, *The Way the World Is*, p.76

'For my thoughts are not your thoughts, neither are your ways my ways,' declares the Lord. 'As the heavens are higher than the earth, so are my ways higher than your ways and my thoughts than your thoughts' (Isa. 55:8-9, NIV).

In our four dimensional world of space-time, Father, Son and Holy Spirit cannot each be individual selves that are each called God and at the same time be constitutive of the one God. However consider the following illustration. In a two dimensional world (a flat surface with no ups or downs), two or more squares are two or more separate things. When they are joined they are no longer squares. However in a three dimensional world (with ups and downs) six squares make one cube. They are joined in a way that could not be imagined in a world on the flat.[12]

When Jesus claimed that God was his Father, the religious leaders objected, saying that he was implying equality with God. They were thinking that Jesus meant there were at least two gods, each self-contained. Jesus replied using completely different concepts, describing his relation with the Father in terms of internal relations such as mutual honouring that constitute what it means to be Father and Son.[13] That mutual honouring between Father, Son and Holy Spirit is an honouring appropriate to

---

[12] I owe this illustration to C.S.Lewis's *Mere Christianity*, Book IV, ch.2.
[13] John 5:17ff.

the relation of being between the Persons of the Trinity. In that relationship (and never one by himself), the Person of each and the whole is constituted and upheld.

A good society is one where we honour one another in ways appropriate to our relationships of being. For example, I give a different love and a different honour to different persons depending on whether the person is my parent, child, teacher, pupil, colleague, employer, employee, husband, wife or friend. In such relationships, each one's true humanity and happiness is discovered.

A Christian alternative to the culture of rights and equality

From the above consideration of the Trinity, we learn that Christian ethics cannot satisfactorily deal with societal problems by simply claiming a human right to equality. Rather must our ethics move on to encourage us in seeking to honour one another in love. It is only in that kind of relationship that we will find our own individual humanity growing to its fruition in Christ. For our sake God himself in the Person of his Son surrendered his rights and entered into our suffering and experienced our death so as to forgive us and lift us up to himself.

Christ did not count his equality with God something to hold on to. He surrendered it for us:

Do nothing out of selfish ambition or vain conceit, but in humility consider others better than yourselves. Each of you should look not only to your own interests, but also to the interests of others. Your attitude should be the same as that of Christ Jesus: Who, being in very nature God, did not consider equality with God something to be grasped, but made himself nothing, taking the very nature of a servant, being made in human likeness. And being found in appearance as a man, he humbled himself and became obedient to death—even death on a cross! Therefore God exalted him to the highest place and gave him the name that is above every name... (Phil. 2:3-9, NIV).

Robert A. Evans, a contemporary writer, tells us:

Human dignity is the foundation for nurturing and protecting human rights. It is rooted in the vision of the 'fullness of life' promised in the incarnation of Jesus Christ and his identification with all humankind. We must be reminded that human dignity is something persons have, not something they must earn or be granted. Dignity is not a quality bestowed on others by the family, by society, or by a government. Rather, dignity is a reality as a consequence of God's good creation and never-ending love.[14]

Human dignity cannot come merely from the doctrine of 'natural law'—based on the belief that we have a good Creator and therefore a good creation. It is the Christian conviction that something has gone wrong with creation. The world is simply not as it ought to be. As we have seen, we cannot get an 'ought' from an 'is'. That is why our understanding

---

[14] *Human Rights in a Global Context.*

of proper human relationships should come from the very nature of God revealed not just in creation, but also in the gospel of the redemption of the world in Christ.

In that gospel we can see that sometimes we are called to surrender our rights and make sacrifices in order that we might help one another. Beyond the sacrifice of Christ is resurrection—a resurrection that embraces all his people and renews their individual humanities in the image of God and in fellowship with one another forever.

CHAPTER NINE

CONCLUSION

Despotism may govern without faith, but liberty cannot.[1]

The continuing atomization of society into selfish units is clearly unsustainable in the long term. As the burden of regulation, fear of litigation, lack of trust, and loss of reason increases, so society increasingly breaks apart. Then we face the danger of a reaction—the reaction of strong government. We are already seeing hints of this in the 'fight against terrorism' where governments are understandably taking away individual freedoms to protect society as a whole. But who or what protects us from government if its powers are misused? The

---

[1] Tocqueville, Alexis Charles Henri Maurice Clérel de (1805-59), French political writer and statesman, whose work on the American political system became a classic. A fuller quotation is: 'Despotism may govern without faith, but liberty cannot.... How is it possible that society should escape destruction if the moral tie is not strengthened in proportion as the political tie is relaxed? And what can be done with a people who are their own masters if they are not submissive to the Deity?' This quotation is taken from his *Democracy in America*, Vol.1, Wordsworth Classics of World Literature, Ware, 1998, Chapter XVII: 'Principal Causes Maintaining The Democratic Republic II'.

media? Some would think that. But how can we be protected from the media's enormous power to shape society's thinking?

When central power gets too great, tyranny is the eventual result. Legislation and a multitude of regulations cannot hold together individual freedom and order. The tyranny may be secular, as was the case in the communist and fascist regimes of the 20th century. On the other hand it might be a religious tyranny that believes God himself is the unknowable great dictator in the sky who merely reveals his commands. In such religion, speaking of God's greatness is to speak of his power to control everything according to his inscrutable will. This kind of religion is bound to encourage the belief that human greatness too is measured in terms of the distant power of an autocrat. Tolerance and democracy are very difficult to maintain is such a belief system.

How different is the religion of the Bible where the source of all goodness seeks, not only that we know his will, but that we know him personally in the loving fellowship of a divine-human family. In that family we are given the 'right' to be his children.[2] Only a society whose moral code recognizes the authority of an eternal Father, Saviour and Judge can

---

[2] 'Yet to all who received him, to those who believed in his name, he gave the right to become children of God' (John 1:12, NIV).

maintain a good balance between freedom and order. There is simply no other way. To those who doubt this, I say: Take a long, hard look at our Western societies; also study world history and the course of the various cultures of its nations and people groups. While Christendom has much in its past of which to be ashamed, nevertheless, when viewed in a world context, countries whose cultures have been deeply infused by the biblical faith stand out for their freedom of thought, advance of experimental science, humanitarian concern and democratic justice. The evidence is overwhelming and is one of the great inductive arguments for the validity of belief in the God of the Christian Scriptures.[3]

To those who fear I am advocating political power for the Christian church please read the appendix.

---

[3] See for example an important conclusion of the influential *Human Accomplishment: The Pursuit of Excellence in the Arts and Sciences, 800 BC to 1950*, by Charles Murray (HarperCollins, London, 2003). Interestingly, not until the end of his research—just a few months before finishing the book, did he reach that conclusion. It was a conclusion he did not expect but he found that the evidence forced him to adopt it.

THE CHURCH, THE CLERGY AND POLITICAL POWER

A widespread complaint

It is common to hear grumbles about the church combining religion with politics instead of getting on with what is perceived to be its real business. It is not only politicians in government—bearing as they do the brunt of the church's censure—but ordinary church members who constantly complain about this.

The response from those clergy who let their political opinions be known is also familiar. They tell us that the Christian message pertains to the whole of life and certainly is concerned with issues of justice which should also be the concern of politicians. Although there seems no answer to that, the feeling of unease among many people continues nonetheless. I confess I share that same unease. Let us, therefore, consider this issue more carefully.

The reason for a Christian concern for politics

Theologically our concern for the world comes from the continuity and discontinuity between this earth and the kingdom of God. Both the biblical testimony to the virgin birth and the resurrection of the body, confirm both God's love for our physical world—a love that we must share—and also the truth that it is only from beyond this world that its salvation comes. This means that Christians have a responsibility to be genuinely concerned with the state of politics in their nation and world. At the same time they recognize that merely reforming this world is never going to solve its problems—God's kingdom must break in from outside. Christians must never give the impression that their main message to the world is political.

The church, the clergy and politics

Could it be that what people are really complaining about is not the church—in its full sense—getting involved in politics, but clergy making political statements and claiming that they are doing so in the name of Christ? Clearly that is a different matter.

Of course the church should be involved in the political life of the nation. It is our hope and prayer that many lay Christians will be involved in parliament, regional and community councils, etc., thus bringing their understanding of the gospel to bear upon the political life of the nation. However, it is not at all clear that the pulpit or the General Assembly or General Synod is the place for political pronouncements.

In the British constitution, the clergy of the two national churches are forbidden from standing for election to parliament. Historically, in the Bible priests and kings were not allowed to combine their functions. When King Saul and later King Uzziah broke this rule, attempting to incorporate priestly functions into their royal office, they faced serious consequences. Most probably the reason for this restriction was that it was recognized that political power, though necessary for the life of any nation, tends to corrupt, and the church's role as the bearer of the gospel to the nation must not be compromised in this way.

Only the One who would be free from sin—and therefore free from a tendency to corrup-tion—could combine the roles of priest and king. That Person was the Messiah and of course his kingdom is 'not of this world'.

However the state does recognize that the church's message and the behaviour of the leaders of the nation are intertwined. Over past centuries, it has demonstrated this by explicitly putting the power of the monarch under the authority of God in the coronation, by giving certain bishops seats in the House of Lords, and by the sovereign always sending a representative to the General Assembly of the Church of Scotland.

Grace not law the true basis for the welfare of communities

There is often a major unspoken assumption in much church contribution to political debate. It is the theory that governments have it in their power to be the great providers of freedom, happiness, employment and prosperity for all. This is to make the fundamental theological error of giving law priority over grace. Surely it should be the other way round. Apart from external defense (armed forces) and internal security (police, courts, etc.), governments are also in the business of legislating to keep us from harming and exploiting one another. This also pertains to the business of taxation and spending in order to provide for all basic education and health care, financial support for the needy, housing provision and schemes for family credit.

In any human society there has to be, on the one hand, personal trust, generosity, kindness, neighbourly concern (that is, grace and faith) and also, on the other hand, legislation and state sponsored welfare (that is, law). However grace is supreme and eternal. Law and nation states are temporary expedients to restrain the chaos that can too easily be caused by human selfishness and sinfulness. The more trust and generosity there is, the less need there will be for law and taxation. Conversely the less personal trust there is the more law will be needed to hold the community together.

If there were no trust between us, an infinite number of laws would be needed to provide the necessary cohesion. Of course this is impossible. Therefore a society without any trust is bound to fall apart no matter how well-meaning and wise is its government. Governments can only make laws. They do not have the power to make us trust and love one another.

Resentment and dependency

When the needy go to collect state financial benefit, they do not feel grateful to the taxpayer for the benefit given. The person who is on the other side of the counter and the taxpayer whose money is being used are not giving out of love for those in need but only because they are under a legal obligation. Although we cannot avoid the need for such a system, it does tend to breed both resentment on the part of the taxpayer and dependency on the part of the recipient. Enormous corruption and inefficiency, involving clever avoidance of tax by the rich and also the bleeding of the system by those on the receiving end, are bound to be endemic to such a system.

So much church criticism of government is made on the assumption that governments have it in their power to bring prosperity and welfare to all. Nevertheless, it is only the spiritual fabric of society that provides the necessary love and trust between human beings. Although law is essential, in its comments about politics the church must not give the impression that legislation and taxation/benefits policies have the power to save society from disintegration. In all church statements to government, the priority of grace over law must be absolutely clear. If we do not make that clear we give the impression that we don't actually believe the Christian gospel and we simply degenerate into just one more political pressure group.

Lack of spiritual leadership

The church should be in the business of providing the spiritual fabric necessary for a real caring society to exist. The government, dependent as it is on the power of law and coercion, cannot provide that spiritual dimension to society and therefore rightly looks to the churches for that provision. When the church responds by merely blaming the government for social deprivation, it is putting its faith in law rather than grace. In so doing it is failing the nation. For the church to put all the blame for the state of the nation on politicians when it must share part of the responsibility, is clearly unhelpful.

I believe that it is the hazy appreciation of this failure that leads so many people to complain about the church mixing religion with politics.

The distinctive contribution of the church to national life

Does the above mean that the church should have nothing to say about tyranny and injustice perpetrated by so many governments in the world? What about Dietrich Bonhoeffer, Karl Barth, and the Confessing Church that witnessed so courageously against Hitler and the Nazis? Certainly if theology were to be withdrawn from the public arena it would lead to serious impoverishment.

Yet also its contribution should be distinctive, not merely duplicating what all well-meaning people say. That was the problem with the so-called 'middle axiom' so loved by William Temple, one of the best known of the 20th century Archbishops of Canterbury. William Temple believed it to be self-evident that the church could not be giving its opinions on every area of government policy, but neither should it be restricted to the mere teaching of doctrine.

Temple believed that from its doctrine it could make a link between its teaching and public policy. For example it could tell the government that it was its duty to do its best to make sure that everyone had decent housing, education, health care and financial provision. It could not dictate to the government how these aims might best be realized. This seems reasonable. However the problem with this 'middle axiom' between doctrine and actual legislation was precisely that already alluded to, namely, that it does not need a theologian to say that housing, education and health for all are good aims for any government.

A false elevation of the state

So what about Karl Barth and the Confessing Church? According to Barth himself, his *Church Dogmatics* did more to challenge Nazism than his political pronouncements. I am sure that is right. The root of the evil of Nazism (and indeed Communism) is to elevate the state into the position of God, not accountable to the true God and the Lordship of Christ. It was the belief that the state could solve the world's problems and bring heaven to earth that in fact brought the world nearer to hell than it had ever been in all its history.

Is this not the ultimate irony of a good deal of the church's political comment? So much of it is based on the assumption that the government has the ability and the duty to be the great provider of good community for all. It is this false assumption that has been behind the worst tyrannies the world has known.

The Church's message for national life

Over against the terrible distortion of the role of government by the Nazis, the Confessing Church proclaimed the Lordship of Christ. Is that not the clear and distinctive message that the churches should be making known today? It does not need complicated research and long reports to keep reminding peoples and leaders what is necessary.

The heart of the public message of the church for nations and governments must surely contain the following:

1. There is a God before whom all nations, peoples and governments are eternally accountable.
2. He has made his will for us known in the Ten Commandments and the Sermon on the Mount.
3. Nations ignore these at their peril.
4. There is in human beings a tendency to corrupt themselves. Government policy in regard to censorship and freedom must take this into account.
5. God loves all peoples and at infinite cost to himself has given us, both ordinary people and politicians, a way of forgiveness in Christ.

It is in the exposition of these principles, as they are given to us in the great story in the Bible, that human beings and national governments can get a sense of purpose. It is from a sense of purpose that we understand the value of anything and everything. Without a publicly agreed purpose and value for human life, no morality, including social morality, can survive. It is in this area most of all that the church must not fail the nation and world. If the 'salt of the earth' loses its distinctive savour, what hope is there for the world it is called upon to preserve?

When our Lord began his Sermon on the Mount, there were many different opinions represented among his hearers. These differing political views were bitterly dividing the people of first-century Israel. Many would have been wondering which sides in the many controversies Jesus would align himself with. However, throughout the sermon he didn't even mention the controversies. Did that mean that his message was irrelevant to these disputes? Not at all! His message went right to the heart of his hearers and therefore challenged the deepest motives behind their arguments and struggles.

Almost all sections of the population eventually rejected him, but in his dying he made atonement for our sins and in his resurrection renewed his promise that he would come again at the end of the age to renew all things and save those who in simple faith humbly look to him.

BIBLIOGRAPHY

Atkins, Peter, 'The Limitless Power of Science', *Nature's Imagination*, John Cornwell (ed.) CUP, Cambridge, 1995.

Bethell, Tom, 'Against Sociobiology', *First Things*, 109, New York, January 2001.

Bruce F.F., *Commentary on Romans*, Tyndale Press, London, 1963.

Dawkins R., *The Selfish Gene*, OUP, Oxford, 1989.

Evans, Robert: *Human Rights in a Global Context*. Quoted at the Oxford Gospel and Culture Conference, September 2002. See http://gospelculture.org.uk/human_rights.htm

Glendon, Mary Ann, *Rights Talk: The Impoverishment of Political Discourse*, The Free Press, New York, 1991.

Hume, Cardinal Basil, 'A Life Less Arbitrary', *The Times*, London, December 10, 1998.

Lewis C.S., *The Problem of Pain*, Collins (Fount), London, 1940.

Lewis C.S., *Mere Christianity*, Collins (Fount), London, 1952.

Lord Hailsham, *The Door Wherein I Went*, Collins (Fount), London, 1975.

Miller, Annabel, 'Is fundamentalism in danger of becoming a blanket word for the general repression of human rights?' *The Times*, London, August 29, 1998.

Murray, Charles, *Human Accomplishment: The Pursuit of Excellence in the Arts and Sciences, 800 BC to 1950*, HarperCollins, London, 2003.

Morgan, Patricia, *Marriage-Lite: The Rise of Cohabitation and its Consequences*, The Institute for the Study of Civil Society, London, 2002.

Newbigin, L., *Foolishness to the Greeks*, SPCK, London, 1986.

Nietzsche, Friedrich Wilhelm, *Beyond Good and Evil: Prelude to a Philosophy of the Future*, trans. Walter Kaufmann, Vintage Books, New York, 1989.

Nietzsche, Friedrich Wilhelm, *The Joyful Wisdom*, Ungar Publishing Company, New York, 1973.

O'Donovan, Oliver, *The Desire of the Nations*, CUP, Cambridge, 1999.

O'Neill, Rebecca, *Experiments in Living: The Fatherless Family*, Civitas, London, 2002.

Phillips, Melanie 'Waking to a false dawn of freedom without duty', *The Sunday Times*, January 2, 2000.

Polkinghorne, J., *The Way the World Is*, Triangle Books, SPCK, London, 1983.

Research News and Opportunities in Science and Theology, The Templeton Foundation, February & May, 2001.

Rorty, Richard, 'Human Rights, Rationality, and Sentimentality', *The Yale Review*, October, 1993.

Ruse, Michael, *Evolutionary Naturalism,* Routledge, New York, 1995, first edition.

Russell, Bertrand, *History of Western Philosophy*, Routledge, New York, 1946, first edition, reprinted 1971, 2000.

Rutherford, Samuel, *Lex Rex*, London, 1644. Recent edition, Sprinkle Publications, Harrisonburg, 1982.

Scott, Drusilla, *Everyman Revived: The Common Sense of Michael Polanyi*, Eerdmans, Grand Rapids, 1985.

Smart, J.J.C. & Haldane, J.J., *Atheism and Theism*, OUP, Blackwell, *Oxford*, 1996.

Stannard, Russell, 'All In The Genes?' *The Tablet*, July 15, 2000.

Stove, David, 'A New Religion', Royal Institute of Philosophy, Vol. 67, no. 260.

Taylor, Howard. 'Review of Consilience', *Philosophia Christi*, Vol. 4, No. 1, 2002, Biola University, California.

Torrance, T.F., *Juridical and Physical Law*, Scottish Academic Press, Edinburgh, 1982.

Turner, Harold, *The Roots of Science,* Deep Sight Trust, Auckland, NZ, 1998.

Turner, Harold, *Frames of Mind*, Deep Sight Trust, Auckland, NZ, 2001.

Warnock, Mary, 'Foundations of Morality', pub. The Royal Institute of Philosophy web pages, April 2003.

Wilson, E., *Consilience*, Knopf, New York, 1998.

Witte, John, Jr, 'The Spirit of the Laws, the Laws of the Spirit', in *God and Globalization*, Stackhouse & Browning (eds), Vol. 2, Moorhouse Publishing, Harrisburg, Penn, 2001.